DEAD LAWYERS

And Other Pleasant Thoughts

by WILEY

Random House
New York

All rights reserved under International and Pan-American Copyright Conventions. Published in the
United States by Random House, Inc., New York, and simultaneously in Canada by Random House
of Canada Limited, Toronto.

Most of the cartoons that appear in this work were originally published in various newspapers.

Library of Congress Cataloging-in-Publication Data

Wiley.
Dead lawyers: and other pleasant thoughts / by Wiley. — 1st ed.
p.   cm.
A collection of strips from *Non Sequitur* previously published in
Washington Post and other newspapers.
ISBN 0-679-74441-X
I. Title.
PN6727.W47D43   1993
741.5'973 — dc20   92-56804

Manufactured in the United States of America
24689753
First Edition

To

Victoria Coviello, Danae Razze, and Kate Gibeson,

the lights of my life

IT STARTED OUT LIKE ANY OTHER DAY IN THE CITY. THE AROMA OF FRESHLY BAKED BREAD FILLED THE AIR, THE MORNING DEW GLISTENED ON LAMP POSTS, A BODY LAY LIFELESS IN THE GUTTER.

IN THE TIME-HONORED TRADITION OF CITY DWELLERS, THOSE FIRST ON THE SCENE TOOK ACTION...

...BY CROWDING AROUND THE CORPSE TO GET A BETTER LOOK.

THE ONLOOKERS QUICKLY BECAME THEIR OWN EXPANDING UNIVERSE, AS LATE ARRIVALS CROWDED AROUND TO GET A GLIMPSE AT THE EPICENTER.

SUDDENLY, A SELF APPOINTED VOICE OF REASON BELLOWED...
DON'T JUST STAND THERE GAWKING...SOMEBODY DO SOMETHING!!
...WHICH TRANSLATED AS, "SEARCH THE BODY FOR A WALLET".

There are basic themes to life in the nineties: The perpetual war of the sexes. Lawyers. The economy. Lawyers. Liberal extremists, conservative extremists, religious extremists. Lawyers. The media. And more lawyers.

This collection of cartoons from the comic strip Non Sequitur hits on these themes and is presented in the precise order as they are dealt to us in life—completely at random.

And, as in life, any attempt to make sense of it all could lead to severe brain damage.

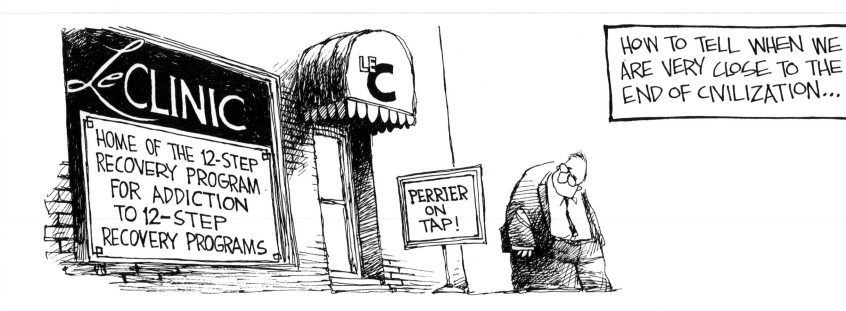

WORD ORIGINS...

HOW TO TELL WHEN YOUR GASOLINE COMES FROM CALIFORNIA...

NOW WITH OAT BRAN

PREMIUM GAS

PIERRE of the NORTH

I HATE ZE YUKON!

ZE NIGHTS ARE ENDLESS, AND EET EEZ ALWAYS SNOWING... I CAN'T THINK OF ONE REASON WHY I SHOULD STAY!

PARDON, MONSIER... DO YOU KNOW ZE WAY TO ZE "NUDES ON ICE" SHOW?

OF COURSE, ZERE IS SOMEZING TO BE SAID FOR ZE HALLUCINATIONS...

...COMEDY HELL...

SIGN of the '80s...

SIGN of the '90s...

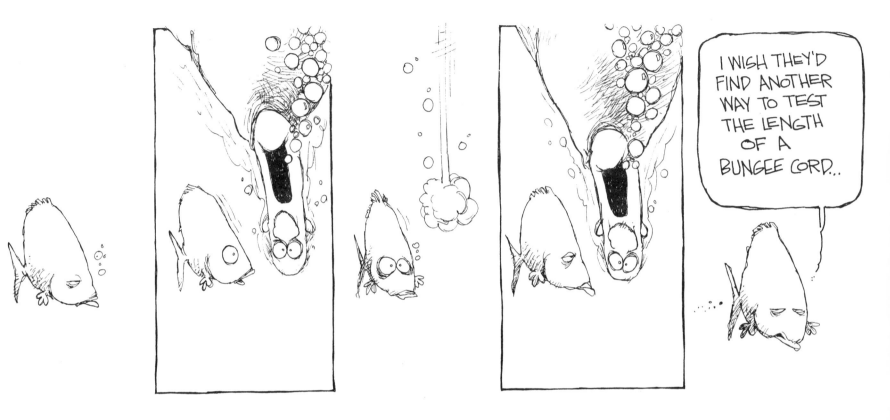

PASSIVE-AGGRESSIVE PIRATES

PLAYING COWBOYS AND INDIANS IN THE '90s...

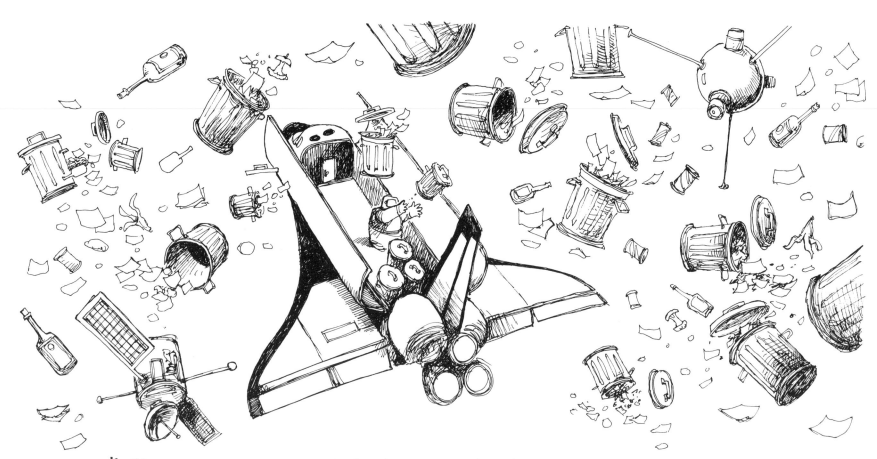

HOW TO TELL WHEN MAN HAS OFFICIALLY CONQUERED SPACE

GRAMMAR TEST

1. USE THE WORD *CONVIVIALITY* IN A SENTENCE.

ANSWER:
The word, "CONVIVIALITY," has never been used in a comic book.

...AND THAT'S WHEN I FIRST REALIZED MY POTENTIAL AS A LAWYER

OK...RING THE SERVANT'S BELL

WHEN RICH GUYS GET BORED...

WHEN CHILDREN of the '60s JOIN the STATUS QUO...

REBEL AGAINST NON-CONFORMITY

HOW TO SPOT A BAD ECONOMIC INDICATOR...

YOU REMEMBER MY STOCKBROKER, DON'T YOU...?

TALENT SHOWS IN THE '90s...

CELL BLOCK B

THE PAROLE BOARD WAS CONVINCED I'D GIVEN UP A LIFE OF CRIME UNTIL I TOLD THEM I PLAN TO BECOME A TELEVANGELIST WHEN I GET OUT...

...WHY YUPPIES ARE THE FIRST TO DISAPPEAR THROUGH NATURAL SELECTION...

MEDICAL DRAMA *in the* NINETIES

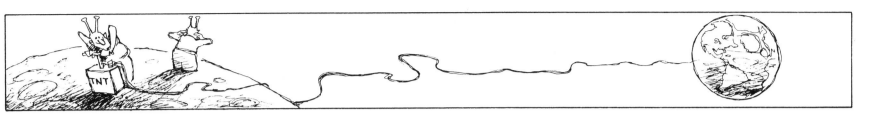

WHY WE EVOLVED **AFTER** THE DINOSAURS

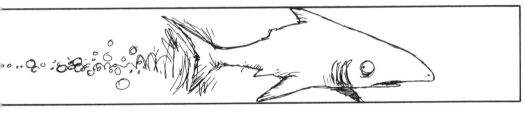

WHY THE AUTOMATIC TRANSMISSION HAD TO BE INVENTED BEFORE THE TIME MACHINE

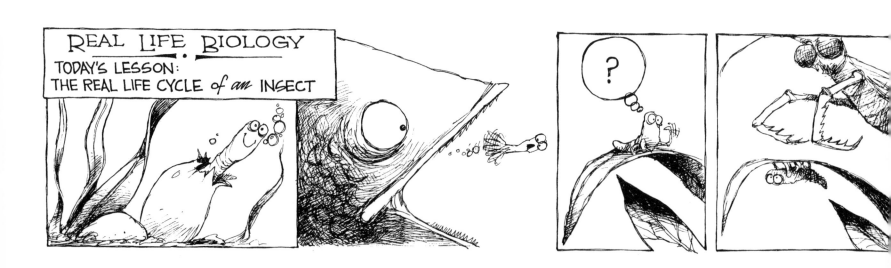

FURTHER EVIDENCE THAT HISTORY IS A MATTER of PERSPECTIVE

I'VE DISCOVERED EUROPEANS!

PROOF of EXTRA-TERRESTRIAL LIFE RESEARCH LAB

EARLY TERM LIMITATIONS...

VOTE FOR ME

VOTE FOR ME AGAIN!

I'M NOT THE INCUMBENT

HOW TO TELL IT'S TIME TO GET A NEW TRAVEL AGENT

...IT SUDDENLY OCCURRED TO ARNOLD THAT HIS REVOLUTIONARY IDEA OF COMBINING WATER AND SNOW SKIING MIGHT NOT BE THE BEST ONE HE EVER HAD...

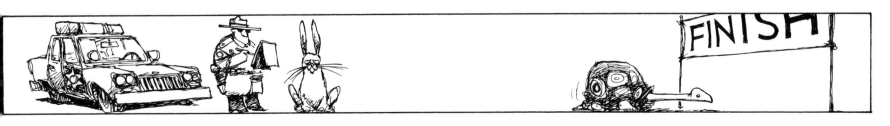

Inventory...December 26th...

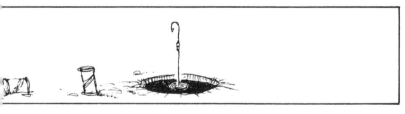

PIERRE of the NORTH

EET EEZ TOO COLD HERE...

ONE OF ZEEZ DAYS I'M GOING TO GET OUT OF HERE AND MOVE TO TAHITI...

OF COURSE, EEF ZEEZ FANTASIES LASTED LONGER, I WOULDN'T NEED TO

TV - STEREO

SUDDENLY, BENNY'S VENTRILOQUIST ACT TOOK AN UGLY TURN...

YEAH...BUT AT LEAST I FINALLY FOUND A JOB WHERE MY PH.D. IN PHILOSOPHY IS PUT TO USE

HE EARNED IT FAIR AND SQUARE. AND AS LONG AS HE'S ABLE TO REPEAT WHAT HE HEARS, HE CAN EARN A DEGREE FROM ANY COLLEGE IN THE COUNTRY

HOW TO SPOT A FUTURE LAWYER

The DAWN of the IRONY AGE...

CONSIDER THE WORLD OF THE ANTS...

THEIR ENDLESS TOIL MAKES THEM MASTERS OF THEIR UNIVERSE

YET THEY SEEM TO BE COMPLETLY UNAWARE OF OUR PRESENCE

THINK OF THE IMPLICATIONS OF OUR RELATIONSHIP TO THEM...

...NATURE'S WAY OF TELLING YOU IT'S TIME TO GO HOME...

SHE ALWAYS SAID THAT SHE WOULDN'T LEAVE HERE UNTIL SHE FOUND "MISTER RIGHT"...

OH, FOR HEAVENS SAKE! AT LEAST GO BRUSH YOUR TEETH!

NEVER BORROW A FLOPPY DISK FROM YOUR EX-WIFE...

AFTER A COUPLE OF HOURS, DR. RAZZE BEGAN TO QUESTION HIS THEORY OF CURING FEAR OF PUBLIC APPEARANCE THROUGH GROUP THERAPY

WHAT ARE YOU WHINING ABOUT? YOU GOT HALF OF WHAT I GOT...

WHY MAFIA LAWYERS DON'T LIKE TO WORK ON CONTINGENCY

TIM IS BROUGHT UP TO SPEED ON WHICH ONE OF HIS REMARKS IS NO LONGER CONSIDERED POLITICALLY CORRECT

SERVING A CABERNET SAUVIGNON WITH WHITE MEAT? GOOD LORD, YOU *ARE* HEATHENS, AREN'T YOU

WHEN SUZANNE STOPPED COMPLAINING ABOUT MEN WHO CAN'T COMMIT...

JUST DATING

...EARLY MAN MOURNS THE PASSING OF THE FIRST LAWYER...

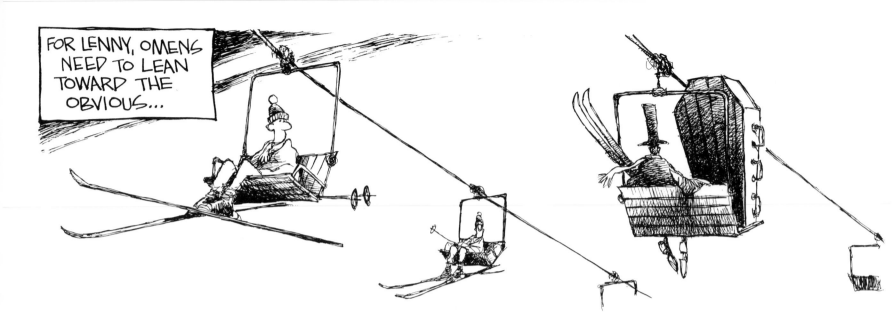

FOR LENNY, OMENS NEED TO LEAN TOWARD THE OBVIOUS...

WHY ESKIMOS STOPPED HAVING GROUND BREAKING CEREMONIES

HOW TO TELL YOUR TRIAL IS GOING TO BE SHORT

WHEN "*KNOW YOUR AUDIENCE*" BECAME THE FIRST RULE OF POLITICAL SATIRE...

THE *OTHER* REASON MOST CORPORATE EXECUTIVES DON'T GET INTO HEAVEN...

COATS AND TIES FORBIDDEN

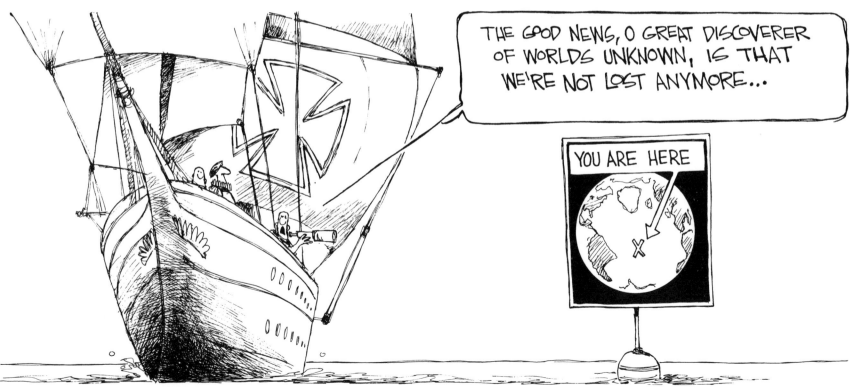

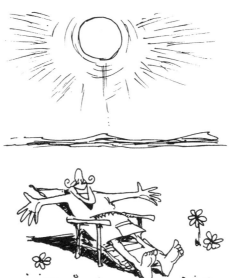

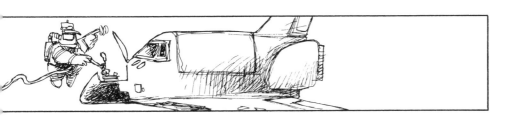

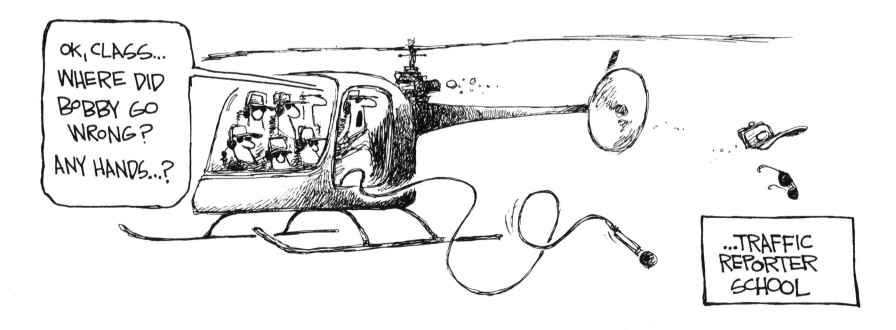

OTHER SIDE of the BLACK HOLE, THEORY #27...

DAMMIT, HE FOUND HIS WAY BACK. THIS TIME I SAY WE PUT HIM IN A BURLAP SACK AND THROW IT IN THE RIVER

PHYSICS AS UNDERSTOOD BY RESTAURATEURS